TRUMP'S TWITTER PRESIDENCY

BY

RUNYARARO NDUDZO

DEDICATION

This book is dedicated to the internet at large. To all those who are interested in politics. Enjoy this book.

BACKGROUND

———

TWITTER

Twitter is one of the major social networks in the world. In late 2017, it was believed to have around 330 million monthly active users and many regard it as the magazine of the world. This platform has attracted many important people including politicians and celebrities who are now using as a way of announcing various developments.

The posts which are put on Twitter are called tweets. Twitter users are limited to 280 words per tweet. This means that tweets are small and often straight to the point. If a tweet get many likes then it is considered to have been successful. A successful tweet also comprises of many retweets. These retweets are a way of sharing anything which has grabbed your attention with your followers. You see unlike other social networks like Facebook where users become friends, on Twitter users don't get friends but followers. A follower is someone who is interested in you but it is up to you whether to follow back or not. You can choose not to follow back and no one will care. So you can have millions of followers and yet you can be following a few users lets say 13.

It is on such a platform that Mr President Mr. D. J Trump is making history putting various tweets which have managed to rock the world.

President Donald J. Trump

Donald J. Trump is the American 45th president who was elected into office in late 2016. Trump is married to Melania Trump, a former model from Slovenia. Trump has five children and eight grandchildren. Two of his children, Donald Jr., Ivanka, and Eric, serve as executive vice presidents of the Trump Organisation.

His ascendancy to power was comedic as most people despised him. YouTubers passed their time by making comedic videos about his candidacy. However like how Hollywood always say, "*there is no such thing as bad popularity*," it turned out that despite the negative vibes Trump was able to win. Leave it to the Americans to decide that a candidate with fewer votes is the winner. However most people have contested the fact that Trump won the elections free and fair. They believe that there was a certain force behind which blew Trump towards being the world leader namely Russia. Russian hackers are believed to have meddled in the American votes swerving the outcome towards Trump. How far true is that?, well I don't know but what I know is that Trump himself has refused such allegations.

Okay enough with the vote rigging stuff. Lets delve deeper into Trump's life and discover who this man was before he started daydreaming about becoming the American president. Almost everyone knows that Trump is a successful businessman. Mr D. J Trump says he started the business with *a small loan* of 14 million. With this he was able to carve a name for himself in the business world. He was able to build the Trump tower and has various TV shows running. However his path to success was not as smooth as you might think. He has certain businesses which failed dismally. The Trump University was a failure and he also failed in the Casino industry. However all in all this man is a successful businessman which may be the main reason why he said that *he will run America like a business* which most of us are yet to see.

"You are fired," are the words which are mostly used when comedians ridicule Trump. Of course they are comedians so most of their content mustn't be trusted but they got this part right. Trump is a no-nonsense guy who is able to fire even the FBI Director. Bad ass right?, I agree with you. However most of the guys who have been fired by Trump were mostly going against his interests. Of course that's why you fire someone in the first place but in this case it may be a little bit different. You see these individuals are serving the American people. So they must be fired if they are not serving the interests of the American people and not when they are investigating allegations of elections rigging and badly want to see your tax returns. So for the record we can say Mr President here is able to bent the law in his favour.

Among many things that Trump is being praised of, keeping a secret is not one of them. If we say Trump likes to brag it will be an understatement, he loves to brag. He loves to brag to the extent that he invited Russian diplomats to the Oval office something unheard of in American history and willingly shared important information acquired from Israel. Anyone who has sailed in the internet waters knows that there is no better place to brag than the social media platforms. So Trump decided to do his bragging on Twitter. They say Mr. president has small hands, but let me assure you that those hands surely know how to type faster than a professional typist as they churn out tweets for the hungry eyes of the world to devour. At the time of writing this book, he has 43.6 million followers. So far he has done a good job of entertaining the world which is always waiting expectantly for his new tweets. Most of Trump's tweets are funny. I mean who doesn't remember the *covfefe* incident which bloggers preached about for days and the comedians speculated about possible meanings of the word. For the record the comedians always testify to the fact that they always love Trump because he keeps them in business.

Social media was an important part of Trump's presidential election campaign in 2016, and was one of the reasons he was ultimately elected. In 2016, his Twitter following exceeded that of his Republican rivals and approached that of his Democratic opponent, Hillary Clinton. Thus Twitter contributed greatly towards the ascendancy of Trump to power.

However Trump had been unfortunate enough to be prevented from banning certain Twitter users. Judge Naomi Reice Buchwald said in her ruling that Trump is violating the U.S. Constitution by preventing certain Americans from viewing his tweets on @realDonaldTrump (Breuninger: 2018). The judge's ruling was in response to a lawsuit filed last July by the Knight First Amendment Institute at Columbia University, as well as seven other plaintiffs whom Trump had personally blocked from following him (Breuninger: 2018).

WHY TWITTER?

IF YOU THINK ABOUT it, why did Trump opt to use Twitter among other way too many social networks?.

MEDIA FILTER

The fact that Donald J. Trump uses the social media to update the nation is not something new as there has been a long tradition of presidents going around the so-called *filter of the press*. This is mainly an effort by presidents to avoid attacks from the Main Stream Media. The media often distort a message through time and at the end the message will be completely different from the original message. As a result most presidents have the urge to divert from the use of the Main Stream Media. They want to speak directly with the people with no middleman. Here are some presidents who have done that.

President Franklin D. Roosevelt delivered his first radio address known later as a fireside chat in March of 1933 in the midst of a crisis of confidence in American banks. The purpose was to reassure the public directly. He would deliver more than two dozen of them over the course of his presidency.

President Dwight Eisenhower did televised fireside chats, held the first televised news conferences and created the White House TV studio.

President Ronald Reagan held prime time news conferences, carried live on network TV.

President Obama's team used social media, releasing its own highly produced videos and posting photos on Flickr rather than letting journalists into the room. And when he needed to sell the Affordable Care Act to young people, Obama sat down "Between Two Ferns" with comedian Zach Galifianakis.

Each president used the latest technology to go around the filter and get directly to the American people in the way that best suited their strengths. For Trump Twitter is the best form of media which he can use. After all his ascendancy to power in a way relied on Twitter. However shortly after winning the election last November, President-elect Donald Trump appeared on 60 Minutes and promised to be more careful in his Twitter use than he was as a candidate. "I'm going to be very restrained, if I use it at all, I'm going to be very restrained," Trump swore (Heer: 2017). However he was not able to keep his promise as he battled with the *FAKE NEWS!,* as he like to call them. Now Trump speaks his mind openly and allows us to covfevferise about his ideas in the comments section.

At the end of the day, each bird has its own distinct sound so why try to mimic a different sound. So he must continue using his twitter account to give unfiltered messages to the populace.

DIVERSIONARY TACTIC

Trump's Twitter use is also regarded by many as a diversionary tactic. The people focus on the petty things whilst the real things they must focus on remain in plain sight and yet they can't see them. Some even think that this Twitter ranting always takes away the seriousness of the issue. People will joke about it and will quickly put it off as they rush to devour the new steamy tweet from Trump.

Often times Trump covers up real news on the investigation of the suspected vote rigging by posting controversial tweets. At one time he diverted people from the news of the Russian hacking scam towards Meryl Streep's speech at the Golden Globe Awards. The tweet read, *"Meryl Streep one of the most overrated actresses in Hollywood, doesn't know me but attacked last night at the Golden Globes. She is a..."* Whilst the investigation on Russia meddling in United States elections was closing in, people were fuming about how Trump could possibly lead to an outbreak of a war by bragging about the size of his nuclear button on twitter. So this shows that running a TV show has its own advantages as you know how to control the minds of the people.

BOTTING IT UP

Twitter is the perfect platform for most leaders because they can implement bots which can perform various tasks on your behalf. A growing number of political actors and governments worldwide are employing both people and bots to shape political conversation (Frolle et al: 2015).

These various bots can do tasks like news updating, replying to commenters and can also be used for spamming and hate speech. It has been rumoured that most of Trumps followers are bots which during the campaign had the rigorous task of keeping people engaged.

THE ADVANTAGES OF TRUMP'S TWITTER USE

———

TRANSFORMING THE POLITICAL ARENA

Trump's twitter use is changing the political game as we know it. Our generation has witnessed the rise of phone wielding leaders who tweet their ideas at every opportunity. However that is not what most people were used to. We were used to seeing nicely dressed presidents promise us things which could only be achieved in our dreams. Now the game is different as we get updated through social media platforms like twitter. It helps to make the lies more palatable if you get my stride.

More and more people are starting to use social media. Our social lives are being marred by these social media apps. So for the leaders to lead their people more effectively, they must go where the people are. So this calls for Presidents to use social media apps in order to get their ideas and announcements across to the people. So in a way Trump is paving the path towards active use of social media apps by leaders. On 1 July 2017 Trump sent out a tweet which justified this which went as follows, "My use of social media is not Presidential – it's MODERN DAY PRESIDENTIAL. Make America Great Again!." So in an age of phone wielding presidents and social media attracted zombies this seems acceptable and the right thing to do. So maybe you must say thank you to Mr Trump the next time you meet the man rather than just criticising him for doing something which may benefit you in the long run.

Trump's twitter use is also a great move towards transparency in the governance of the American country. The use of twitter enables the people to know what is going on. You are more connected to the people, I mean it only takes one tweet and in seconds thousands of people would have received the information. So the use of Twitter by Trump is bridging the gap between the leaders and the people.

With the rise of the internet, the world is moving at a faster pace towards globalisation. So in order for the whole world to stay connected people must know what is happening on all four corners of the world. This means that Mr. Trump's twitter use enables the people all over the world to access the statements which he will be making. In a second, the whole world will be able to know his thoughts on many different issues. So when it comes to matters of globalisation, Trump's twitter use is helping.

OPENNESS WITH PEOPLE

Trump's twitter use has created transparency when it comes to the governance of America and International relations. The president tweets every thought and every action which he is about to take. This makes it easy for the people to grasp what is happening before and when it is happening. Compared to the past this is a major improvement as people used to be in the dark.

I have realised that Trump's tweets often create healthy debates on the twitter platform. Of course there are many trolls who just want to criticise everything but I have often seen many policies being debated and many good points being raised. This is something which every policy maker will adore. The people are now being given a voice because of the president's twitter use. This is really steering politics in a good direction.

ENTERTAINMENT

Believe it or not, Trump's twitter use has transformed the entertainment industry. Most comedians like, John Stewart and Trevor Noah now rely on Trump for their content. In the past they had to hunt for content to use in their political satire. However these days, Trump is always supplying them with unique content everyday. That man is full of energy and does many extraordinary things which leaves you wondering if he is even real. However the shows of these comedians are becoming a little stale as they are mainly focusing on Trump.

THE DISADVANTAGES OF TRUMP'S TWITTER USE

PERSONAL

Trump has been robbing his own dignity by using social media mainly through mistypos. Mistypos, oh! You are surprised, then you better strap your seatbelts because it is about to get crazy. You see typing errors are common I mean we do them almost everyday especially on the social media platforms. However for Trump that is different because he is the President. It has been ingrained in humans for a long time that leaders must be perfect. They must do everything by the book, follow the expectations of the society and act as role models. The bottom line is, leaders mustn't make mistakes. However Trump's Twitter use has landed him in trouble many times over typo errors. A good example is the covfefe incident which most took advantage of in order to ridicule the president thereby tarnishing his image. The Washington post of May 31 2017 claimed that the tweet was liked and retweeted over a hundred thousand times, making it one of the most popular tweets of 2017 to that date, as people speculated on the meaning of "covfefe." It seems funny doesn't it that the word which broke down the internet came from a president.

However for the mistypos can we blame the president alone. Well luckily I like pointing fingers and I think those close to the president must be blamed for letting this happen. I mean as the president of America you mean you can't find one person who looks over such petty things. It is my understanding that those close to the president have a job of maintaining a perfect image of the president. The White House also stated that the president's tweets must be regarded as official statements. This means that there is much at stake here. Thus there must be a system set up for filtering the bad message from Trump's tweets rather than letting him loose because when that guy goes on a tweeting spree, then the security of the American country will most likely be jeopardized. At the moment they suck at that job so they need to step up their game.

I think that the social media world is not conducive for leaders. You see it is part of the free world where the motto is, *do what thoust like.* This means that everyone is open to criticism whether you do the right thing or not. That place has people who only live to give negative comments for. So it goes without saying that anyone who want to be respected must avoid social media platforms.

TARNISHING AMERICAN IMAGE

Trump has been engaged in many twitter fights. These have tarnished the image of the American president thereby tarnishing the image of America itself. Among these fights is Trump's fight with Michael Moore.

Most people have considered kicking Trump off Twitter. They believe that this will restrict him from making stupid comments

GIVES PRESIDENTS FREE REIGN

The relationship between the president and the people wont be that effective if the president likes to use a virtual megaphone. Trump is known for putting various policy making thoughts on his Twitter feed. However this is less effective as there will be a lack of serious communication between the leader and the people. Policy making has also been disrupted. Although policies are credited to have been made by presidents, these policies take a long time to make and are made after many deliberations by various officials. However because of the use of Twitter, Trump is now able to bypass those officials and make foreign policies on his own. This of course will result in the making of foreign policies which will always prove to be disastrous.

Direct communication with the people by presidents will also result in many lies by the presidents. The Founders didn't want the president to make direct appeals to the people, and for a while presidents rarely did. George Washington averaged three popular speeches a year; John Adams, one; James Madison, zero. I don't know how many tweets Trump averages per day, but I know it's more than zero, which is too many. To paraphrase George Will, there is in Trump an inverse relationship between the confidence he has in tweeting his thoughts and the care he takes in forming them. This means that constant direct communication with the people is always disastrous as questionable information can get out. So the Americans must really consider banning their president from using the twitter platform.

FOREIGN POLICY

The American history may be tarnished as the people will learn about a president who seemed off. Elizabeth Landers noted that the Former White House Press Secretary Sean Spicer said during his tenure that Trump's tweets are "considered official statements by the President of the United States". If so then this means that what Trump is doing is hurting the country. He is always picking fights with other world leaders on Twitter. This creates more problems for America's foreign policy and it clearly means that Mr. Trump must be stopped before doing any damage.

The continued use of twitter by Trump is negatively affecting America's foreign policy. Most of Trump's tweets are against foreign diplomats which is buying America more enemies than friends. Even the friends are not doing what friends must really do as they are afraid that Mr. President may accidentally type them on his phone and put them up on his twitter feed.

Trump declared war on North Korea on the 23rd of September 2017. In the tweet the President said, "Just heard Foreign Minister of North Korea speak at U.N. If he echoes thoughts of Little Rocket Man, they won't be around for much longer." Well this was not wrong at all because the Americans are known for their urge to blow things up. However this bypassed many Government procedures which must be taken before you threaten another country. So Twitter in the hands of presidents can bring about the advent of the Third World War.

Trump's tweets have also targeted allies of the United States thereby weakening relationships. After the June 2017 London attack, Mayor of London Sadiq Khan condemned it and said that "the city remains one of the safest in the world" and there was "no reason to be alarmed" over the increased police presence around the city. The latter comment was criticized by Trump in a tweet: "At least 7 dead and 48 wounded in terror attack and Mayor of London says there is no reason to be alarmed!"

This of course was a major blow on the American's foreign policy. How can allies depend on a person who laughs on their efforts to solve their problems in times of trouble.

COMPANIES AFFECTED

When it comes to big businesses, stocks can plummet or flourish based on a number of factors most of which the company wont be able to control. Trump has also been a reason behind many companies successes and failures.

"Toyota Motor said will build a new plant in Baja, Mexico, to build Corolla cars for U.S. NO WAY!" Trump tweeted in January. "Build plant in U.S. or pay big border tax." Toyota's stock promptly fell. This shows that Trump's twitter account now holds unimaginable powers over companies. There's even an app that lets you know when Trump has tweeted negatively about a publicly traded company, so you can sell quickly if needed. Another company created a lightning-fast Twitter bot that automatically short sells such stocks. It's called "Trump and Dump."

EFFECTS TO TWITTER

———

IF TRUMP IS LEADING anything, then its the Social Media world. He is very good on criticising all those who go against him and is not hesitant to use foul language when he believes that it is necessary. He knows fully well that he cannot be banned and he takes advantage of it. He insults people using foul words which includes telling them that they have bleeding faces and how he never call them short and fat. Because he is the Twitter president, no one does anything and we just watch as the president lashes out with his virtual sword striking down his opponents.

MORE USERS

The dream of every social platform is to get more users. Trump in a way has fulfilled this dream for the twitter platform. His use of twitter is now attracting many people to the platform who want to see his typos first hand. His use has also formalised the use of twitter for political debates. Many politicians all over the world have joined the platform and are utilising it to the fullest. All this is benefiting twitter which makes Trump more of a hero

LONGEVITY

As time goes on, most social media platforms tend to lose users. A good example is Facebook which lost many users because of privacy issues. Although most people postulate that all social networks are birds of the same feathers, the love which this platform is receiving from politicians will definitely ensure that it will stay popular for a long time.

SOLUTION

KICKING OUT

Most Americans have realised that Trump is ruining their country's prestige through his Twitter use and they want him off the site. According to a June 2017 Fox News poll, 70 percent of respondents said Trump's tweets were hurting his agenda and 17 percent said the tweets were helpful. This clearly shows that Trump's twitter use is humiliating Americans as most of these tweets are questionable. Even those close to Trump are said to be advising him to put down his phone and do things the old way.

Most people have speculated that the continued use of Twitter by Trump distracts him form his duties as the American president. This has led to many Americans being opposed to Trump's Twitter use. According to a new ABC News/Washington *Post* poll. About 67% of Americans disapprove of the way Trump uses Twitter, the poll found. When asked to describe the President's Twitter usage, about 68% found Trump's tweets "inappropriate," 65% described the tweets as "insulting," while 52% called it "dangerous." This shows that Trump's actions on Twitter is not being liked by most Americans. So in a way Trump has made the people aware that the use of Social media by leaders may prove to be dangerous.

The people close to Trump have also considered restricting his twitter use because the unrestricted use is causing more harm than is necessary. The CNN article of 3 December 2017 noted that Donald Trump's tweet last weekend about fired national security adviser Michael Flynn sparked consideration among the President's staff of imposing new rules on how messages are posted on his social media accounts amid consternation by his aides and lawyers, according to sources familiar with the situation. "I've been pretty candid with him and all of you that I'm not a fan of the daily tweets," Senate Majority Leader Mitch McConnell told reporters earlier this year.

It may seem as if Trump is putting his full weight on Twitter and it is not able to ban him. Donald Trump has been violating Twitter's "rules" for years. He has been the platform to insult individuals, entire ethnic groups and yet he has not been kicked out. Lee *et al* noted that as of November 2017, Trump had insulted 394 people, places, and things on Twitter, ranging from politicians to journalists and news outlets to entire countries On September 25, Twitter co-founder Biz Stone finally addressed the issue in a short tepidly-written piece on Medium. The statement written reflected the fact that for Trump's sake, the platform was going to review its policy in order to meet Trump's twitter needs. The Twitter team has also shown that Trump's tweeting in an a way benefits the country which means that he wont be banned anytime soon.

What Trump is doing is not politically wrong so why ban him. Emma Llanso, director of the Center for Democracy & Technology's Free Expression Project, said Trump's tweets are "very clearly politically relevant speech" and are even being cited in court cases challenging the president's policies. For example, a U.S. appeals court used Trump's tweets in June to block his travel ban on people from six predominantly Muslim countries.

EMBRACING

As much as most will like to deny it, Trump's twitter use has many benefits which we have discussed above. As a result we must embrace the presence of the president on the platform after all he is a modern president.

CONCLUSION

THE CONTINUED PRESENCE of Trump on Twitter and his popularity on the platform clearly makes him a twitter president. The twitter presidency is clearly wreaking havoc both locally and internationally. Trump engages in various twitter wars which undermines his dignity as president.

However the president's twitter use has some advantages as it is transforming the political arena as we know it. There is now better engagement with the general and more transparency which ensures that the public will trust the government.

REFERENCES

ANDREWS, TRAVIS M. (May 31, 2017). *Trump targets 'negative press covfefe' in garbled midnight tweet that becomes worldwide joke*. The Washington Post. Archived from the original on May 31, 2017. Retrieved May 31, 2017.

Blanton, Dana (June 29, 2017). *Fox News Poll: Voters say Trump's tweets hurting agenda*. Fox News. Archived from the original on July 2, 2017. Retrieved July 3, 2017.

Breuninger. K and Mangan. D, *Trump can't block Twitter followers, federal judge says,* https://www.cnbc.com/2018/05/23/trump-cant-block-twitter-followers-federal-judge-says.html

Elizabeth Landers (June 6, 2017). *Spicer: Tweets are Trump's official statements*. CNN. Archived from the original on July 20, 2017.

Forelle,M. C. et al, *"Political Bots and the Manipulation of Public Opinion in Venezuela,"* Project on Computational Propaganda, Oxford, UK, Working Paper 2015.1, Jul. 2015

Heer. J, *The case for taking Trump's tweets seriously,* https://newrepublic.com/article/141233/case-taking-trumps-tweets-seriously, March 9, 2017

Lee, Jasmie C.; Quealy, Kevin (November 29, 2017). *The 394 People, Places and Things Donald Trump Has Insulted on Twitter:*

A Complete List. The New York Times. Archived from the original on September 29, 2017. Retrieved November 29, 2017.\

Maegan Vazquez et al. (December 3 2017), *Trump's lawyer says he was behind President's tweet about firing Flynn*, CNN article retrieved on 14 January 2017

Don't miss out!

Visit the website below and you can sign up to receive emails whenever Runyararo Ndudzo publishes a new book. There's no charge and no obligation.

https://books2read.com/r/B-A-GTEF-KHFY

BOOKS 2 READ

Connecting independent readers to independent writers.